Rollin C. Ward

Crown Him for Revival Meetings, Sabbath Schools and General Church Services

Rollin C. Ward

Crown Him for Revival Meetings, Sabbath Schools and General Church Services

ISBN/EAN: 9783337270001

Printed in Europe, USA, Canada, Australia, Japan

Cover: Foto ©Lupo / pixelio.de

More available books at **www.hansebooks.com**

"CROWN HIM."

FOR

REVIVAL MEETINGS

SABBATH SCHOOLS

AND

GENERAL CHURCH SERVICES.

BY

ROLLIN C. WARD, D. M.

PUBLISHED BY

THE R. C. WARD CO.,

CANTON, OHIO. AND MIDDLE BRANCH, OHIO.

THE UNITED BRETHREN PUBLISHING HOUSE,

DAYTON, OHIO.

Copyright, 1893, by R. C. Ward.

PREFACE.

COME, let us sing unto the Lord:
Riches and honor He'll bestow
On all whose trust is in his word,
Which guides our pathway here below.
Nor will He ever turn aside
His child, that needs his constant care;
In all His wisdom He will guide
Me to that home, so bright and fair.

With the earnest prayer that this collection of songs shall be instrumental in leading thousands to "Crown Him Lord of All," it goes forth on its mission of Good.

Very truly,

R. C. WARD.

CANTON, OHIO, December 1, 1883.

"Crown Him."

No. 1.   "Crown Him."

EDWARD PERRONET, 1780.   R. C. WARD.

1. { All hail the pow'r of Jesus' name, Let angels prostrate fall;
     Bring forth the royal diadem, And crown Him Lord of all.
2. { Let ev'ry kindred, ev'ry tribe, On this terrestrial ball,
     To Him all majesty ascribe, And crown Him Lord of all.
3. { Oh! that with yonder sacred throng, We at His feet may fall,
     We'll join the everlasting song, And crown Him Lord of all.

CHORUS.
We will crown Him, Yes, we'll crown Him, Give to
We will crown Him Lord of all, Yes, we'll crown Him Lord of all, Give to
Jesus all the glory, Hallelujah; We will crown Him,
Jesus all the glory, all the glory, Hallelujah, We will crown Him Lord of all.
Yes, we'll crown Him.
Yes, we'll crown Him Lord of all, We will crown the Savior Lord of all.

Copyright 1892, by R. C. Ward.

No. 2. Call Them In.

ANNA SHIPTON. R. C. WARD.

1. "Call them in!"—the poor, the wretched, Sin-stain'd wand'rers from the fold.
2. "Call them in!"—the Jew, the Gen-tile, Bid the strangers to the feast,
3. "Call them in!"—the bro-ken hearted, Cow'ring 'neath the brand of shame;

Peace and par-don free-ly of-fer: Can you weigh their worth with gold?
"Call them in!" the rich, the no-ble, From the high-est to the least.
Speak love's message, low and tender, "'Twas for sin-ners Je-sus came."

"Call them in!" the weak and wea-ry, La-den with the doom of sin;
Forth the Fa-ther runs to meet them, He hath all their sorrows seen;
See! the shadows lengthen round us, Soon the day-dawn will be-gin;

CHO. *"Call them in," the poor, the low-ly, Sick and foot-sore, stain'd with sin;*

D.S. for Chorus, FINE.

Bid them come and rest in Je-sus, He is wait-ing, "call them in!"
Robe and ring, and roy-al sandals Wait the lost ones, "call them in!"
Can you leave them lost and lonely? Christ is com-ing, "call them in!"

Je-sus died to pay their ransom. He is wait-ing, "call them in!"

Words from "Woman in Sacred Song." By per. Eva Munson Smith.

My Sure Foundation. Concluded.

Je - sus, my sure Foun-da - tion, Sav-ior, Pro-tec - tor, Friend.

No. 7. To Whom Shall I Go?

VIOLET E. KING.   A. S. EYMAN.

1. To whom shall I go, blessed Lord, When billows of sin o'er me roll?
2. To whom shall I go, blessed Lord, For help un-to whom shall I call,
3. To whom shall I go, ah! Thy words In answer, come sweetly to me;
4. To whom shall I go, when the dews Of death's night shall gather around?

There is none but Thee who can cheer And comfort the pen-i - tent soul.
When weary of life and its toil? To Thee, who art all and in all.
Come, all who are la - den with care, And rest I will give un - to thee.
With Thee in yon beau-ti - ful home, At last may my spir- it be found.

CHORUS.

Un-to Thee would I go, And within Thy sweet presence a-bide.
Un-to Thee would I go, blessed Lord,

Thou a-lone art a rock and defense, In whom I can safely con-fide.

Used by Permission.

No. 13. Come To The Fountain.

O. W. Slusser.

1. There is a fountain filled with blood, Drawn from Immanuel's veins And sinners plung'd beneath that flood, Lose all their guilty stains.
2. The dying thief re-joiced to see, That fountain in his day, And there may I, tho' vile as he, Wash all my sins a-way.
3. E'er since by faith I saw the stream, Thy flowing wounds supply. Redeeming love has been my theme, And shall be till I die

CHORUS.
Come to this fountain, to-day, Come to this fountain, to-day; to-day, Jesus has promis'd to cleanse from all sin, Will you come to this fountain today?

No. 14. Key of G.

1 How tedious and tasteless the hours,
 When Jesus no longer I see!
Sweet prospects, sweet birds and sweet flowers,
 Have all lost their sweetness to me.
The midsummer sun shines but dim,
 The fields strive in vain to look gay;
But when I am happy in Him,
 December's as pleasant as May.

2 His name yields the richest perfume,
 And sweeter than music His voice;
His presence disperses my gloom,
 And makes all within me rejoice:
I should, were He always thus nigh,
 Have nothing to wish or to fear;
No mortal so happy as I,—
 My summers would last all the year.

3 My Lord, if indeed I am Thine,
 If Thou art my sun and my song,
Say, why do I languish and pine?
 And why are my winters so long?
Oh, drive these dark clouds from my sky!
 Thy soul cheering presence restore;
Or take me to Thee up on high,
 Where winter and clouds are no more.

No. 16. The Water of Life.

Oh, For A Thousand tongues Concluded.

No. 18. Key of A.

1 Oh, think of the home over there,
By the side of the river of light,
Where the saints all immortal and fair,
Are rob'd in their garments of white,
REF.—Over there, over there,
Oh, think of the home over there.

2 Oh, think of the friends over there,
Who before us the journey have trod,
Of the songs that they breathe on the air
In their home in the palace of God
REF.—Over there, over there,
Oh, think of the friends over there.

3 My Savior is now over there, [rest.
There my kindred and friends are at
Then away from my sorrow and care,
Let me fly to the land of the blest. REF.

The Flowing Fountain. Concluded.

No. 22. Where Are Your Treasures?

No. 23. Home Mission Hymn.

Mrs. W. W. McNair. R. C. Ward.

1. Wave, wave the Gos-pel banner, With cross and crim-son line,
2. Take it, ye sons and daughters, That from our fire-sides go,
3. Be-hold! the thronging na-tions, Pour in on ev-'ry side,
4. Tell them of tru-er free-dom, Re-lease from Sa-tan's chain,

Un-furl to ev-'ry sin-ner This sig-nal so di-vine;
Plant it be-side your al-tars, Fear not the sight of foes;
They come form Or-ient re-gions, And coun-tries far and wide,
Pro-claim the roy-al ran-som, Je-sus for sin-ners slain;

Wave it on Rock-y Moun-tains, On old Pa-cif-ic's shore,
In U-tah and Wy-o-ming, Far to the set-ting sun,
From Chi-na's flow-'ry king-dom, From E-rin's blooming Isle,
His name is on our ban-ner, A-bove the cross it shines,

By flow-ing stream and fountain, And low-ly cab-in door.
Keep still our en-sign wav-ing, Till vic-to-ry is won.
They hear the voice of free-dom, And flee from bondage vile.
Be-hold it! ev-'ry sin-ner, It glows in liv-ing lines.

CHORUS.

Wave, wave the Gos-pel ban-ner, With cross and crim-son line,

Words from "Woman in Sacred Song." By per. Eva Munson Smith.

No. 25. Welcome Morn.

ANNA C. BARBAULD. R. C. WARD.

1. A-gain the Lord of life and light, Awakes the kindling ray Un-
2. Oh, what a night was that Which wrapt The heathen world in gloom! Oh,
3. And still for err-ing, guil-ty men, A brother's pi-ty flows; And

seals the eye-lids of the morn, And pours in-creas-ing day, Ten
what a sun which broke this day, Tri-umph-ant from the tomb! Je-
still His bleed-ing heart is touched With mem-'ry of our woes, To

thous-and lips u-nit-ed Shall hail this wel-come morn, Which
sus! the friend of sin-ners, With strong com-pas-sion moved, De-
Thee, my King and Sav-ior, Glad hom-age let me give; And

scat-ters blessings from its wings To na-tions yet un-born.
scend-ed, like a pit-ying God, To save the souls He loved.
stand prepared, like Thee, to die, With Thee that I may live.

CHORUS.
Wel-come morn of life and beau-ty,

Welcome morn of joy and gladness, Morn of life and beau-ty, Let

Words from "Woman in Sacred Song." By permission of Eva Munson Smith.

Will The Waters Be Chilly? Concluded

3 When at last o'er the river,
  Safely landed I stand,
  Robed in beauty Eternal,
  And my harp within my hand;
  I will join in the chorus,
  With the ransomed ones above,
  Hallelujah forever!
  Jesus reigns, the God of love.

No. 30. Come With A Message.

LAURA E. NEWELL.   C. E. LESLIE.

1. Come with a message from Jesus, Words could not be more sweet,
2. Come with a message from Jesus, When from the loved I part;
3. Come with a message from Jesus, Should I be led to sin;
4. Come with a message from Jesus, When I approach death's stream,

Whisper His love to my spirit, Jesus, my soul's retreat.
Tell how His presence shall comfort, Comfort my aching heart.
When there's confusion about me, Sorrow and doubt within.
When all earth's trials are over, Ending life's fitful dream,

Come when the sunshine with splendor Gleameth on all around,
Tell of His peace and His pardon, Pity and home and rest;
Tell of His strength and His mercy, How He can still uphold,
Whisper His sweet words of comfort: I would not be dismayed,

Come with a message from Jesus, Dearest friend ever found.
Come with a message from Jesus, When I am sore oppressed.
Guide thro' temptation to safety, All who will seek His fold.
Could He but speak to my spirit, "'Tis I, be not afraid."

From "Heavenly Tidings." Used by per. of C. E. Leslie.

The Parting Hand. Concluded.

4 And since it is God's holy will
We must be parted for a while,
In sweet submission, all as one,
We'll say, "Our Father's will be done,"
My youthful friends in christian ties,
Who seek for mansions in the skies,
Fight on, we'll gain that happy shore,
Where parting will be known no more.

5 And now, my friends, both old and young,
I hope in Christ you'll still go on;
And if on earth we meet no more,
Oh, may we meet on Canaan's shore!
I hope you'll all remember me,
If you no more on earth I see,
An interest in your prayers I crave,
That we may meet beyond the grave.

There Awaits a Crown. Concluded.

No. 38.

1 Majestic sweetness sits enthroned,
  Upon the Savior's brow;
  His head with radiant glory crowned,
  His lips with grace o'erflow.

2 No mortal can with Him compare,
  Among the sons of men;
  Fairer is He, than all the fair
  Who fill the heavenly train.

3 He saw me plunged in deep distress,
  And flew to my relief,
  For me He bore the shameful cross,
  And carried all my grief.

4 To heaven, the place of His abode,
  He brings my weary feet;
  Shows me the glories of my God,
  And makes my joys complete.

No. 39. Sweetly Saved.

Dr. B. T. Yohe. R. C. Ward.

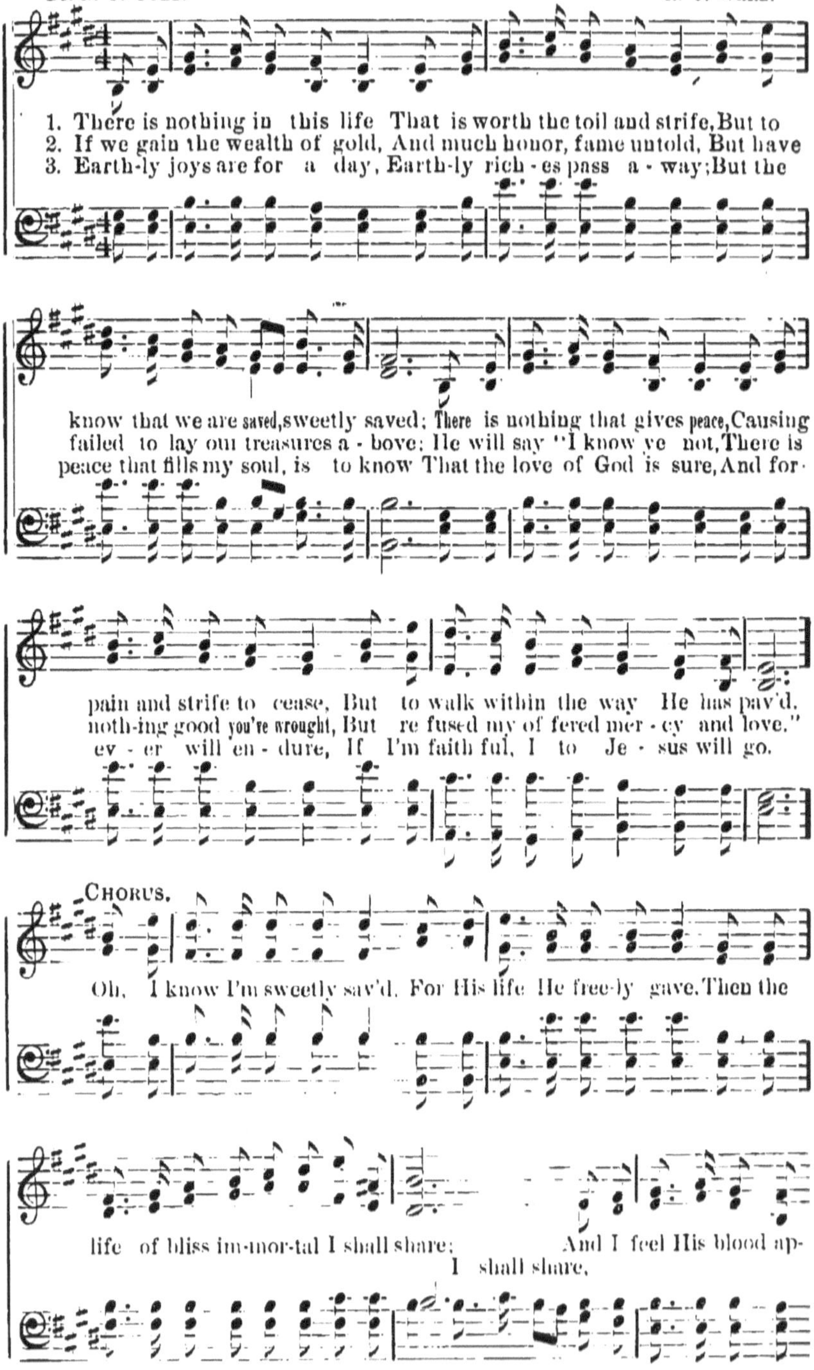

1. There is nothing in this life That is worth the toil and strife, But to
2. If we gain the wealth of gold, And much honor, fame untold, But have
3. Earth-ly joys are for a day, Earth-ly rich-es pass a-way; But the

know that we are saved, sweetly saved; There is nothing that gives peace, Causing
failed to lay our treasures a-bove; He will say "I know ye not, There is
peace that fills my soul, is to know That the love of God is sure, And for-

pain and strife to cease, But to walk within the way He has pav'd.
noth-ing good you're wrought, But re fused my of-fered mer-cy and love."
ev-er will en-dure, If I'm faithful, I to Je-sus will go.

CHORUS.

Oh, I know I'm sweetly sav'd, For His life He free-ly gave. Then the

life of bliss im-mor-tal I shall share; And I feel His blood ap-
I shall share,

No. 41. Rock Of Ages.

Copyright, 1893, by R. C. Ward.

Rock Of Ages. Concluded.

The Whole Wide World. Concluded.

"The cross of Je-sus" at our side, We'd con-quer by and by.

Ring out the joy-ous sound, Let hills and vales re-sound;

The whole wide world for Christ, Till all have His sal-va-tion found.

No. 47. Come To Jesus.

English.

1. Come to Je-sus, come to Je-sus, Come to Je-sus, just now, Just now, come to Je-sus, come to Je-sus, just now.

2 He will save you.
3 Oh, believe Him.
4 He is able.
5 He is willing.
6 He'll receive you.
7 Call upon Him.
8 He will hear you.
9 Look unto Him.
10 He'll forgive you.
11 Flee to Jesus.
12 He will cleanse you.
13 He will clothe you.
14 Jesus loves you.
15 Don't reject Him.
16 Only trust Him.
17 Hallelujah, Amen.

No. 48. Jerusalem, My Glorious Home.

E. L. WHITE.
Arr. with Chorus by R. C. WARD.

1. Je - ru - sa - lem, my glo - rious home! Name ev - er dear to me!
2. Oh, when, thou cit - y of my God. Shall I thy courts as-cend,
3. Why should I shrink at pain and woe? Or feel at death dis may?

When shall my la - bors have an end. In joy, and peace, and thee?
Where con-gre - ga - tions ne'er break up, And Sab - baths have no end?
I've Canaan's good - ly land in view, And realms of end - less day.

When shall these eyes thy heaven-built walls And pearly gates be - hold?
There hap - pier bow'rs than E - den's bloom, Nor sin nor sor - row know:
Je - ru - sa - lem, my glo - rious home! My soul still pants for thee;

Thy bulwarks with sal - va - tion strong And streets of shining gold?
Blest seats! thro' rude and storm - y scenes, I on -ward press to you.
Then shall my la - bors have an end. When I thy joys shall see.

CHORUS.

long for the home of the blest. To walk thro the

I long for the home of the blest, To walk thro' th' streets of

Copyright, 1893, by R. C. Ward.

No. 51. Fill My Heart With Gladness.

Dr. B. T. Yohe.   R. C. Ward.

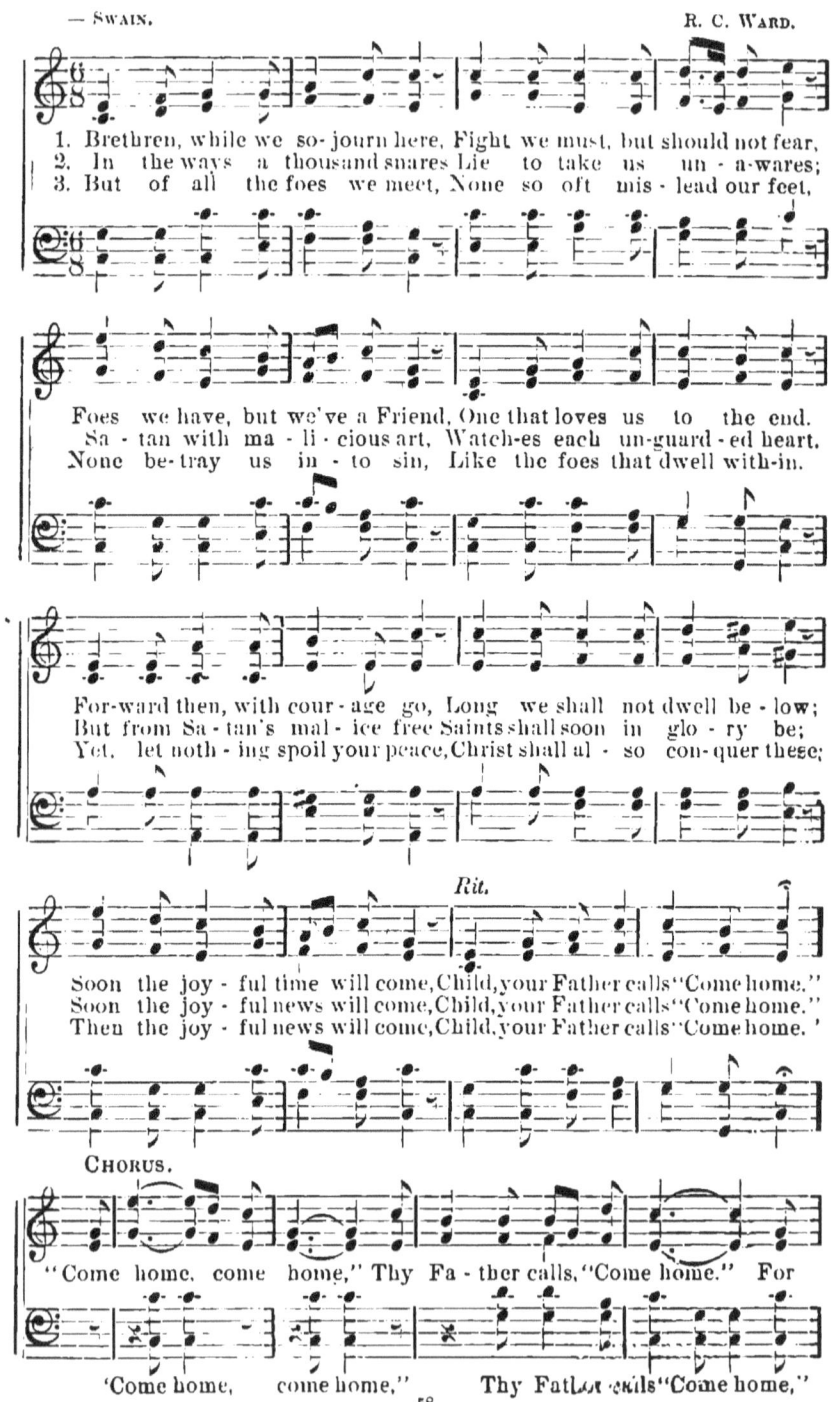

No. 55. Sinner, He Calls Thee.

R. C. W.   R. C. WARD.

1. Je - sus is ten - der - ly call-ing thee Home from the paths of sin;
2. Long hast thou wandered o'er mountains bare, Far from the Shepherd's fold;
3. Man - y the bless-ings He off - ers thee; On - ly ac - cept and live.
4. Won-der-ful mer - cy that flows so free! Wonderful love He gave!

Plead-ing so ten - der - ly, "Sin-ner come," Je-sus will take you in.
Come to that cit - y of end - less day, Paved with the purest gold.
Come with your sins, at His foot-stool bow, Ten-der - ly He'll for - give.
Won-der-ful peace that a - bides with-in! Won-der-ful grace to save.

CHORUS.

Then come, O come; His mer - cy is boundless and free,
Then come, O come,   and free;

He waits to save, And ten - der-ly calls for thee.
He waits to save,

No. 56. Christians' Battle Song.

R. C. W.   Old melody arr by R. C. Ward.

1. Rouse ye, Chris-tian sol-diers, hear the call to-day.
2. In this might-y bat-tle wa-ging fierce and strong,
3. When the smoke of bat-tle all is cleared a-way

Du-ty bids you for-ward, why de-lay? Sa-tan with his ar-my
Je-sus leads the for-ces 'gainst the wrong. Courage, then, my brother,
And the shades of dark-ness turn'd to day; Seat-ed on His throne all

seeks to put to shame The fol-low'rs of the Sa-vior's name.
nev-er say dis-may, For God is with the right to-day.
ra-di-ant and bright Ap-pears the spot-less Prince of Light.

While the care-less sol-dier slum-bers in his tent,
Fol-low, then, your Lead-er, where-so-e'er the call,
Clothed in robes of white, with palms of vic-to-ry,

Heed-ing not the call from heaven sent, Stead-i-ly the foe moves
While you heed His voice you can not fall, Gird-ing on your ar-mor,
Comes the shi-ning host from land and sea, Shout-ing un-to Him who

Copyright, 1893, by R. C. Ward.

Christians' Battle Song. Concluded.

No. 57.

1 Oh, happy day, that fixed my choice
  On Thee my Savior and my God;
Well may this glowing heart rejoice,
  And tell its raptures all abroad.

2 Oh, happy bond, that seals my vows
  To Him who merits all my love!
Let cheerful anthems fill the house,
  While to the altar now I move.

3 'Tis done—the great transaction's done;
  I am my Lord's, and He is mine;
He drew me, and I followed on,
  Rejoiced to own the call divine.

4 Now rest—my long divided heart
  Fixed on this blissful center, rest—
Here have I found a nobler part,
  Here heavenly pleasures fill my breast.

5 High heaven, that heard the solemn vow,
  That vow renewed shall daily hear;
Till, in life's latest hour, I bow,
  And bless in death a bond so dear.

Cho.—Happy day! happy day!
  When Jesus washed my sins away;
He taught me how to watch and pray
  And live rejoicing every day.
Happy day! happy day!
  When Jesus washed my sins away.

No. 58. The Little Builders.

MARIA A. WEST. R. C. WARD.

1. Lit-tle buil-ders all are we, Buil-ders for e-ter-ni-ty;
2. One by one the stones we lay, Buil-ding slow-ly day by day;
3. Build-ing in vast Chi-na, too, Liv-ing tem-ples rise to view;
4. On Mount Leb-a-non's fair heights, By our ma-ny gathered mites;

Chil-dren of the mis-sion bands, Working with our hearts and hands
Build-ing by our love are we, In the lands be-yond the sea;
Build-ing in Ja-pan as well, Ah! what sto-ries we could tell!
Where the Nile's sweet wa-ters pour, Build-ing all the wide world o'er;

Build-ing tem-ples for our King, By the of-fer-ings we bring;
Build-ing by each tho't and prayer For the souls that suf-fer there;
Build-ing on dark Af-ric's shore, That there may be slaves no more.
And one day our eyes shall see, In a glad e-ter-ni-ty,

Liv-ing tem-ples He doth raise Filled with life and light and praise.
Build-ing in the Hin-doo land, Where the i-dols are as sand.
Build-ing in the Turks doomed land, For Ar-me-nia's scattered band.
"Liv-ing stones" we helped to bring For the pal-ace of our King.

Words from "Woman in Sacred Song." By permission of Eva. Munson Smith.

The Little Builders. Concluded.

CHORUS.
We are build-ers for our King; Un-to Him our prais-es bring,
Hap-py lit-tle build-ers we, Build-ing for e-ter-ni-ty.

No. 59. There'll Be No Sorrow There.

MARY S. B. DANA, 1850. E. W. DUNHAM, 1851.

1. Oh! sing to me of heaven, When I am called to die;
2. When cold and slug-gish drops Roll off my mar-ble brow,
3. When the last mo-ments come, Oh! watch my dy-ing face,
4. Then to my rap-tured ear Let one sweet song be given;

Cho. There'll be no sor-row there, There'll be no sor-row there.

D. C. for CHORUS.

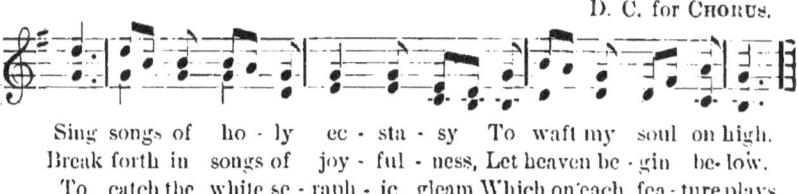

Sing songs of ho-ly ec-sta-sy To waft my soul on high.
Break forth in songs of joy-ful-ness, Let heaven be-gin be-low.
To catch the white se-raph-ic gleam Which on each fea-ture plays.
Let mu-sic cheer me last on earth, And greet me first in heaven.

In heaven a-bove, where all is love, There'll be no sor-row there.

No. 61. Christian Soldiers.

I. Watts, 1723.   R. C. Ward.

1. Am I a sol-dier of the cross, A fol-lower of the Lamb?
2. Must I be car-ried to the skies, On flow'-ry beds of ease,
3. Are there no foes for me to face? Must I not stem the flood?
4. Sure I must fight if I would reign; In crease my cour-age, Lord!

And shall I fear to own His cause, Or blush to speak His name?
While oth-ers fought to win the prize, And sailed thro' blood y seas?
Is this vile world a friend to grace, To help me on to God?
I'll bear the toil, en-dure the pain, Sup-port-ed by Thy word.

CHORUS.

We will fight for the cause of the Mas - ter, We will
We will fight for the cause of the Mas - ter,

work in His vine-yard to-day; We will
We will work in his vine-yard to-day;

la-bor to bring ma-ny souls to Him, Who wan-der far a-way.
We will

The Resurrection. Concluded.

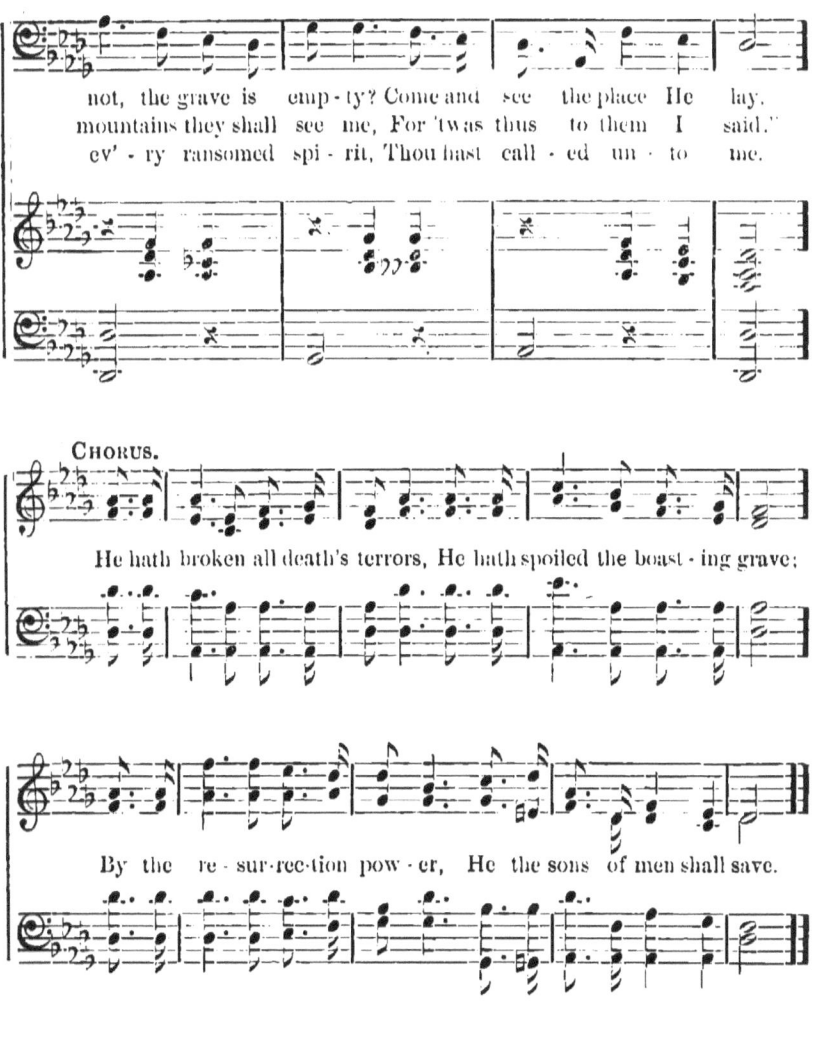

not, the grave is emp-ty? Come and see the place He lay.
mountains they shall see me, For 'twas thus to them I said."
ev' - ry ransomed spi - rit, Thou hast call - ed un - to me.

CHORUS.

He hath broken all death's terrors, He hath spoiled the boast-ing grave;
By the re - sur-rec-tion pow - er, He the sons of men shall save.

No. 69.

1 Simply trusting every day,
Trusting through a stormy way;
Even when my faith is small,
Trusting Jesus, that is all.

CHO. Trusting Him while life shall last,
Trusting Him till earth is past,
Till within the jasper wall—
Trusting Jesus, that is all.

2 Brightly doth His spirit shine
Into this poor heart of mine;
While He leads I cannot fall,
Trusting Jesus, that is all —CHO.

3 Trusting as the moments fly,
Trusting as the days go by,
Trusting Him, whate'er befall—
Trusting Jesus, that is all.—CHO.

No. 70. The Same Sweet Story.

Mrs. Adaline H. Beery.   Geo. F. Rosche.

1. We sing of Christ our Sav-ior, And how he came be-low
2. We sing the gra-cious par-don That brought us to the light;
3. We sing His crown-ing mer-cy, His death to make us free;

To build His bless-ed king-dom And seeds of good-ness sow.
And how He helps His ser-vants Who trust His love and might.
His glo-rious res-ur-rec-tion, Blest hope for you and me.

CHORUS.

We sing on earth His glo - ry, And when in heav'n we share,

Repeat Chorus pp.

We'll sing with hal - le - lu - jahs The same sweet sto - ry there.

Used by per. of Geo. F. Rosche, owner of the copyright. Chicago, Ill.

No. 71. We're Going Home.

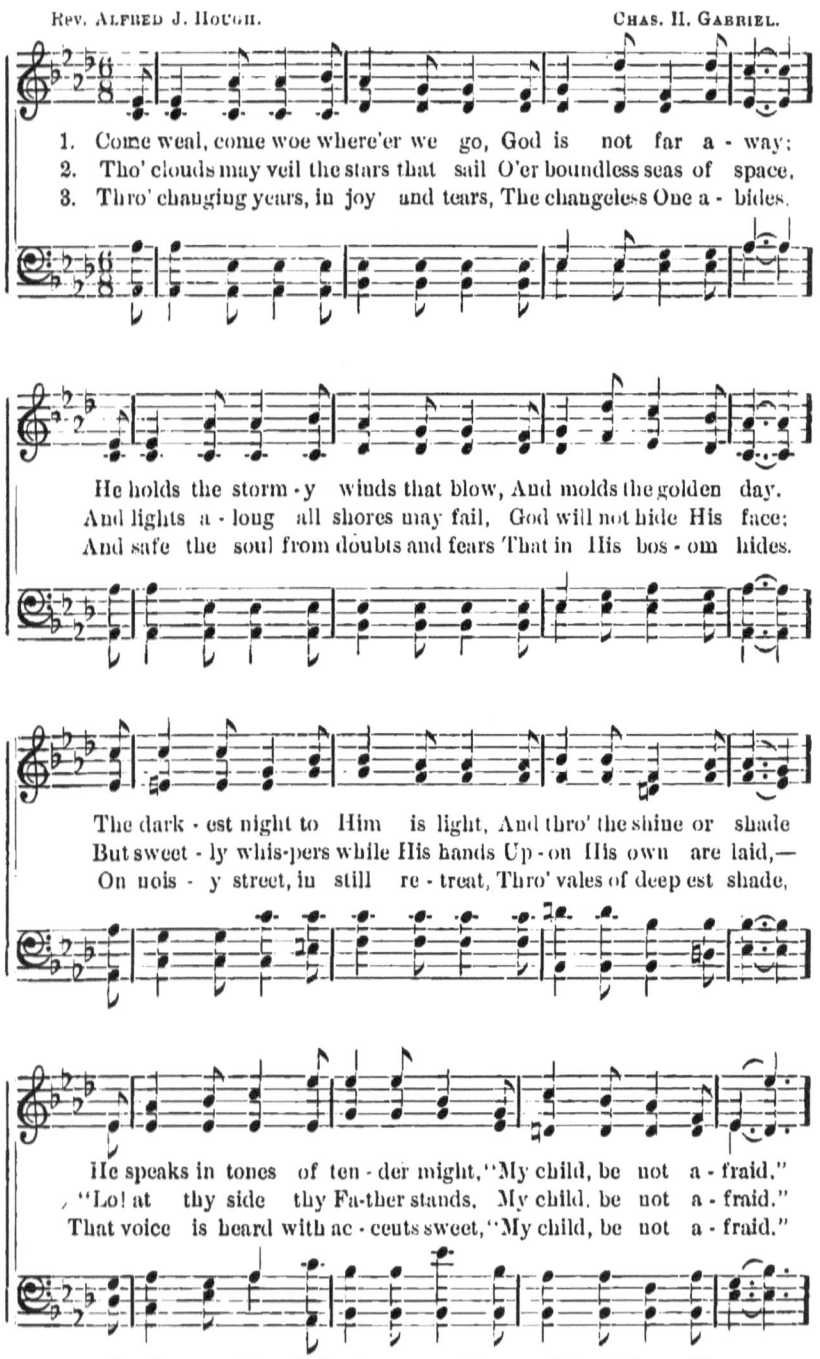

Be Not Afraid. Concluded.

No. 73.

1. Children of the heavenly King,
As we journey let us sing;
Sing our Savior's worthy praise,
Glorious in His works and ways.

2. We are trav'ling home to God,
In the way our fathers trod;
They are happy now, and we
Soon their happiness shall see.

3. Fear not; brethren, joyful stand
On the borders of our land;
Jesus Christ, our Father's Son,
Bids us undismayed go on.

4. Lord! obediently we'll go,
Gladly leaving all below;
Only Thou our leader be,
And we still will follow Thee!

No. 75. He Keepeth Me, Ever.

E. R. Latta.   Geo. F. Rosche.

1. He keepeth me, ev-er, Wher-e'er be the place! I've on-ly to ask it— Most won-der-ful grace! Though sor-est temp-ta-tions My spir-it may try. I know my Re-deem-er Will ev-er be nigh!

2. He keepeth me, ev-er, With ten-der-est care! I've on-ly to ask Him My bur-dens to bear! A word of His promise He nev-er will break! Who-ev-er may leave me, He ne'er will for-sake!

3. He keepeth me, ev-er, From yielding to dread; Tho' darkness be round me, And clouds o-ver-head! He still-eth my doubtings, He light-ens my grief! I've on-ly to trust Him— He'll give me re-lief!

Chorus.

He keepeth me, ev-er! His love end-eth nev-er! From Him naught shall sev-er! He keepeth my soul!

Used by per. of Geo. F. Rosche, owner of the copyright. Chicago, Ill.

The Transfiguration. Concluded.

CHORUS.

Oh, the glory of the vis-ion Seen by mor-tals here be-low!
Tell the world the wondrous sto-ry, Thus His dy-ing love be-stow.

No. 77. Behold the Lamb of God!

A. J. ASHE.   R. C. WARD.

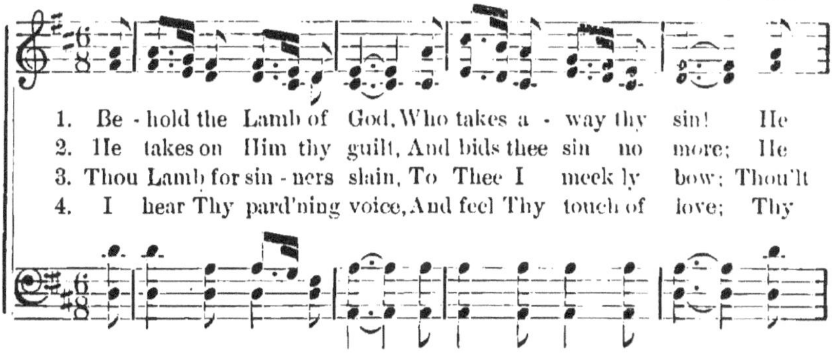

1. Be-hold the Lamb of God, Who takes a-way thy sin! He
2. He takes on Him thy guilt, And bids thee sin no more; He
3. Thou Lamb for sin-ners slain, To Thee I meek-ly bow; Thou'lt
4. I hear Thy pard'ning voice, And feel Thy touch of love; Thy

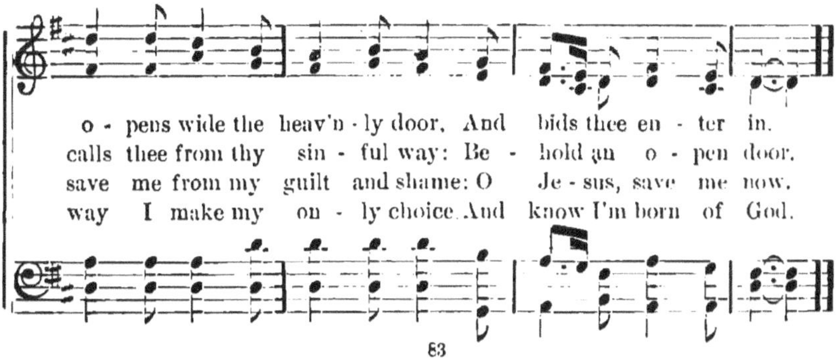

o-pens wide the heav'n-ly door, And bids thee en-ter in.
calls thee from thy sin-ful way: Be-hold an o-pen door.
save me from my guilt and shame: O Je-sus, save me now.
way I make my on-ly choice, And know I'm born of God.

Galilee. Concluded.

dread;.......... And say, "'Tis I, be not a-fraid."
and all my dread; "be not afraid."

No. 83.   Millennial Morn.

SARAH C. GOUGHNOUR. R. C. WARD.

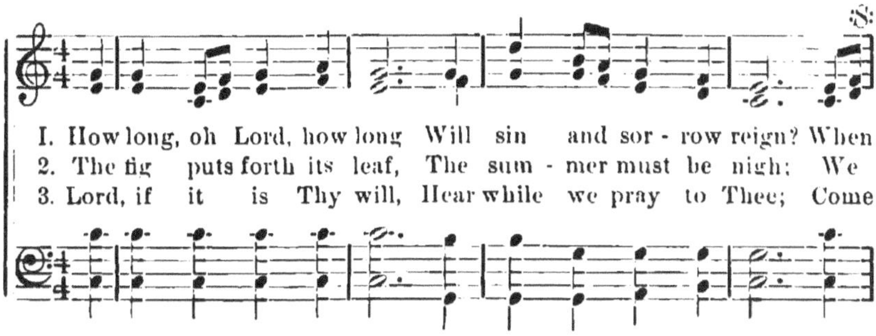

1. How long, oh Lord, how long Will sin and sor - row reign? When
2. The fig puts forth its leaf, The sum - mer must be nigh; We
3. Lord, if it is Thy will, Hear while we pray to Thee; Come

will the sweet mil - len - nial morn Bring peace to earth a - gain?
pray Thee help our un - be - lief, And hear us when we cry.
near and whis-per,"Peace be still And calm the troub - led sea.

REFRAIN. D.S.

Bring peace to earth a - gain, Bring peace to earth a - gain.
And hear us when we cry, And hear us when we cry.
And calm the troub-led sea, And calm the troub - led sea.

No. 84. Self Consecration.

RAY PALMER.   O. W. SLUSSER.

1. Take me, oh, my Father! take me, Take me, save me, thro' Thy Son;
2. Long from Thee my footsteps straying, Thorny proved the way I trod;
3. Fruitless years with grief re-calling, Humbly I confess my sin;
4. Freely now to Thee I proffer This relenting heart of mine;

That which Thou would'st have me, make me, Let Thy will in me be done.
Weary come I now, and praying—Take me to Thy love, my God!
At Thy feet, O Father! falling, To Thy household take me in.
Freely, life and soul I offer—Gift unworthy love like Thine.

CHORUS.

Father! take me, all forgiving; Fold me to Thy loving breast;
In Thy hope for-ev-er living, I must be for-ev-er blest!

No. 85.

1 Oh, for a closer walk with God,
  A calm and heavenly frame;
  A light to shine upon the road
  That leads me to the Lamb.

2 Return, O holy Dove, return,
  Sweet messenger of rest;
  I hate the sins that made Thee mourn,
  And drove Thee from my breast.

3 The dearest idol I have known,
  Whate'er that idol be,
  Help me to tear it from Thy throne,
  And worship only Thee.

No. 86. I'm Nearer My Home.

Used by per. of Geo. F. Rosche, owner of the copyright. Chicago, Ill.

The Old-Fashioned Way. Concluded.

No. 88.

1 Blest be the tie that binds
  Our hearts in Christian love;
  The fellowship of kindred minds
  Is like to that above.
2 Before our Father's throne
  We pour our ardent prayers;
  Our fears, our hopes, our aims are one,
  Our comforts and our cares.
3 We share our mutual woes,
  Our mutual burdens bear;
  And often for each other flows
  The sympathising tear.

No. 89. Safe On The Shining Strand.

LAURA E. NEWELL.   D. W. CRIST.

1. Oh! the white-robed throng On the shining strand, Oh! the grand "new song"
2. Sweet the peace-ful rest, When the toil is done, Then all strife shall cease,
3. Lo! the sun-set tints, Light the west-ern sky, For the day is past,
4. Oh! the white robed throng On the shining strand, Sweet the grand "new song"

Of the an-gel band, When the gold-en harps, Sweet-est
And a crown be won, Oh! the home sweet home, Oh! the
And the night is nigh, But His voice calls soft, O'er death's
Of the an-gel band, Soon we'll sing with them That ex-

tones re-sound, When the word comes home, That "the lost is found!"
joys that wait When we en-ter in, At the pearl-y gate.
storm-y sea, "I will bear thee home, On-ly trust in Me."
ult-ant strain, With our loved and lost, We shall meet a-gain.

CHORUS.

Oh! the white-robed angel band,   Oh! that home beyond the sea,
         angel band,   o'er the sea,

Safe up-on the shining strand,...... There my loved ones wait for me.
         shin-ing strand,

From "Banner of Love." By per.

No. 94.

1 Come, Holy Spirit, heavenly Dove,
  With all Thy quick'ning powers;
 Kindle a flame of sacred love
  In these cold hearts of ours.

2 Dear Lord! and shall we ever live
  At this poor dying rate,
 Our love so faint, so cold to Thee,
  And Thine to us so great?

3 Come, Holy Spirit, heavenly Dove,
  With all Thy quick'ning powers;
 Come shed abroad a Savior's love,
  And that shall kindle ours.

No. 97. What Must It Be To Be There.

Mrs E. Mills.   J. C. Ewing.

1. We speak of the realms of the blest, That country so bright and so fair,
2. We speak of its pathways of gold, Its walls decked with jewels so rare,
3. We speak of its freedom from sin, From sorrow, temptation and care,

And oft are its glories confessed: But what must it be to be there!
Of wonders and pleasures untold; But what must it be to be there!
From trials without and within: But what must it be to be there!

CHORUS.

To be there, to be there; O what must it be to be there!
To be there, to be there.
To be there, to be there, O what must it be to be there.
To be there, to be there.

4 We speak of its service of love,
  The robes which the glorified wear,
The Church of the First-born above:
  But what must it be to be there!

5 O Lord, in this valley of woe,
  Our spirits for heaven prepare;
Then shortly we also shall know
  And feel what it is to be there.

Copyright, 1883, by J. C. Ewing. Used by per.

It Can Never Be Told. Concluded.

No. 99. Help Me, Savior.

Dr. B. T. Youe.   R. C. Ward.

1. Dear Sav-ior, help me to be true And faith-ful un-to Thee;
2. Oh help me oth-ers to for-give As Thou dost par-don me;
3. Yes, ev-'ry mo-ment, ev-'ry hour; I need Thee ev-'ry day;

100 WHEN THE KING COMES IN.

J. E. LANDOR.   E. S. LORENZ.

1. Called to the feast by the King are we, Sit-ting, perhaps, where his peo-ple be, How will it fare, friend, with thee and me
2. Crowns on the head where the thorns have been, Glo-ri-fied he who once died for men, Splen-did the vis-ion be-fore us then,
3. Like lightning's flash will that instant show Things hidden long from both friend and foe, Just what we are will each neigh-bor know,
4. Joy-ful his eye shall on each one rest Who is in white wedding gar-ments dressed, Ah well for us if we stand the test,

REFRAIN.

When the King comes in?
When the King comes in. When the King comes in, brother, When the King comes
When the King comes in.
When the King comes in.

in! How will it fare with thee and me When the King comes in?

5 Endless the separation then,
  Bitter the cry of deluded men,
  Awful that moment beyond all ken,
  When the King comes in.

6 Lord, grant us all, we implore thee, grace,
  So to await thee each in his place,
  That we may fear not to see thy face
  When thou comest in.

101. THOU THINKEST, LORD, OF ME.

E. D. MUND.   "The Lord thinketh upon me."—Ps. 40: 17.   E. S. LORENZ.

1. A-mid the tri-als which I meet, A-mid the thorns that pierce my feet,
2. The cares of life come thronging fast, Upon my soul their shad-ow cast;
3. Let shadows come, let shadows go, Let life be bright or dark with woe,

One thought remains supreme-ly sweet, Thou thinkest, Lord, of me!
Their gloom reminds my heart at last, Thou thinkest, Lord, of me!
I am con-tent, for this I know, Thou thinkest, Lord, of me!

CHORUS.

Thou thinkest, Lord, of me, (of me,) Thou thinkest, Lord, of me, (of me,)
What need I fear since thou art near, And thinkest, Lord, of me.

Copyright, 1885, by E. S. Lorenz.

No. 105. Responsive Service. Consecration.
Opening Invocation.

Rev. JOHN R. CALGAN.—Devotional.   A. F. MYERS. By per.

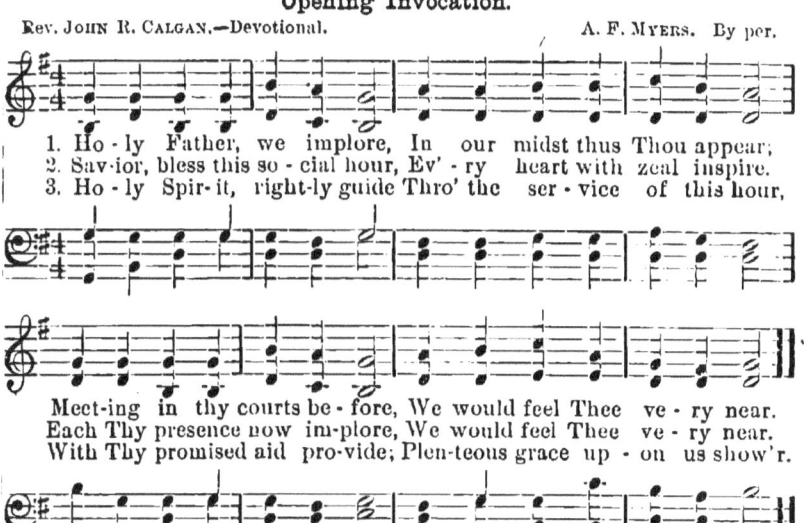

1. Ho-ly Father, we implore, In our midst thus Thou appear;
2. Sav-ior, bless this so-cial hour, Ev'-ry heart with zeal inspire.
3. Ho-ly Spir-it, right-ly guide Thro' the ser-vice of this hour,

Meet-ing in thy courts be-fore, We would feel Thee ve-ry near.
Each Thy presence now im-plore, We would feel Thee ve-ry near.
With Thy promised aid pro-vide; Plen-teous grace up-on us show'r.

LEADER—

Who then is willing to consecrate his service this day unto the Lord?

CONGREGATION—

I beseech you, therefore, brethren, by the mercies of God, that ye present your bodies a living sacrifice, holy, acceptable unto God, which is your reasonable service.

LEADER—

For ye are bought with a price: therefore glorify God in your body, and in your spirit, which are God's.

Sing, on opposite page, Verse 1, "Take my heart, dear Jesus," etc.

LEADER—

As ye have yielded your members servants to uncleanness and to iniquity unto iniquity; even so now yield your members servants to righteousness unto holiness.

CONGREGATION—

Know ye not, that to whom ye yield your-selves servants to obey, his servants ye are to whom ye obey; whether of sin unto death, or of obedience unto righteousness?

LEADER—

He died for all, that they which live should not henceforth live unto themselves, but unto Him which died for them, and rose again.

Sing—Verse 2, "Take my heart, dear Jesus."

LEADER—

Thou shalt love the Lord thy God with all thy heart, and with all thy soul, and with all thy strength, and with all thy mind; and thy neighbor as thyself.

CONGREGATION—

Whether therefore ye eat, or drink, or what-soever ye do, do all to the glory of God.

LEADER—

No man can serve two masters: for either he will hate the one, and love the other; or else he will hold to the one, and despise the other. Ye cannot serve God and mammon.

CONGREGATION—

And when they had brought their ships to land, they forsook all, and followed Him.

Sing—Verse 3, "Take my heart," etc.

No. 106. Responsive Service. ^{Grace.}

Opening Song No. 16, "The Water of Life."

Leader—
And now, brethren, I commend you to God, and to the word of His grace, which is able to build you up, and to give you an inheritance among all them which are sanctified.

Congregation—
For the law was given by Moses, but grace and truth came by Jesus Christ.

Sing—Verse 1, "Grace! 't is a charming," etc.

Leader—
Being justified freely by His grace through the redemption that is in Christ Jesus.

Congregation—
By whom also we have access by faith into this grace wherein we stand, and rejoice in hope of the glory of God.

Leader—
Hath God forgotten to be gracious? hath He in anger shut up His tender mercies?

Congregation—
But Thou, O Lord, art a God full of compassion, and gracious, long-suffering, and plenteous in mercy and truth.

Sing—Verse 2, "Grace first contrived," etc.

Leader—
He hath made His wonderful works to be remembered: the Lord is gracious, and full of compassion.

Congregation—
And therefore will the Lord wait, that He may be gracious unto you; and therefore will He be exalted, that He may have mercy upon you: for the Lord is a God of judgment: blessed are all they that wait for Him.

Leader—
Grace be unto you, and peace, from God our Father and from the Lord Jesus Christ.

Sing—Verses 3 and 4.

No. 107. Dennis.

Philip Doddridge. H. G. Nageli.

1. Grace! 'tis a charming sound, Harmonious to the ear!
Heav'n with the echo shall resound, And all the earth shall hear.

2 Grace first contrived a way
   To save rebellious man:
  And all the steps that Grace display,
   Which drew the wondrous plan.

3 Grace led my roving feet
   To tread the heav'nly road;
  And new supplies each hour I meet,
   While pressing on to God.

4 Grace all the work shall crown,
   Thro' everlasting days,
  It lays in heav'n the topmost stone,
   And well deserves the praise.

No. 108. Responsive Service. Work.

Opening Song — No. 56.

Leader —
Son, go work to-day in My vineyard

Congregation —
He that believeth on Me, the works that I do shall he do also; and greater works than these shall he do; because I go unto my Father.

Leader —
Glory, honor, and peace, to every man that worketh good.

Congregation —
Ye shall know them by their fruits. Do men gather grapes of thorns, or figs of thistles? Even so every good tree bringeth forth good fruit; but a corrupt tree bringeth forth evil fruit.

Sing — Verse 1, "Must Jesus bear," etc.

Leader —
Wherefore, my beloved, , work out your own salvation with fear and trembling: for it is God which worketh in you both to will and to do of His good pleasure.

Congregation —
Let your light so shine before men, that they may see your good works, and glorify your Father which is in heaven.

Leader —
Then said they unto Him, What shall we do, that we might work the works of God?

Congregation —
Jesus answered and said unto them, This is the work of God, that ye believe on Him whom He hath sent.

Leader —
Study to show thyself approved unto God, a workman that needeth not to be ashamed.

Sing — Verses 2 and 3

No. 109. Maitland.
G. N. A.   G. N. Allen.

1. Must Jesus bear the cross a-lone, And all the world go free? No there's a cross for ev'ry one, And there's a cross for me.

2 How happy are the saints above.
  Who once went sorrowing here!
  But now they taste unmingled love,
  And joy without a tear

3 This consecrated cross I'll bear.
  Till death shall set me free.
  And then go home my crown to wear
  For there's a crown for me.

No. 110. Responsive Service. Love.

Opening Song, No. 9, "The Story will Never Grow Old."

LEADER—
This is my commandment, That ye love one another, as I have loved you.
CONGREGATION—
Who shall separate us from the love of Christ? shall tribulation, or distress, or persecution, or famine, or nakedness, or peril, or sword?
LEADER—
The law of the Lord is perfect, converting the soul: the testimony of the Lord is sure, making wise the simple.
Sing—Verse 1, "Lord! what a heaven," etc.
LEADER—
That Christ may dwell in your hearts by faith; that ye, being rooted and grounded in love, may . . . know the love of Christ, which passeth knowledge, and that ye might be filled with all the fullness of God.
CONGREGATION—
Walk in love, as Christ also hath loved us, and hath given Himself for us, an offering and a sacrifice to God for a sweet-smelling savor.

LEADER—
Thou shalt love the Lord thy God with all thy heart, and with all thy soul, and with all thy mind.
CONGREGATION—
He that hath My commandments, and keepeth them, he it is that loveth Me: and he that loveth Me shall be loved of My Father, and I will love him, and will manifest myself to him.
Sing—Verse 2, "When I can say," etc.
LEADER—
Let love be without dissimulation. Abhor that which is evil; cleave to that which is good.
CONGREGATION—
Whoso keepeth His word, in him verily is the love of God perfected: hereby know we that we are in Him.
LEADER—
A new commandment I give unto you, That ye love one another; as I have loved you, that ye also love one another. By this shall all men know that ye are my disciples.
Sing—Verse 3, "While such a scene of," etc.

No. 111. Loving Kindness.

ISAAC WATTS. Western Melody.

1. Lord! what a heaven of saving grace Shines thro' the beauties of Thy face, And lights our passions to a flame! Lord! how we love Thy charming name!

CODA.
Loving-kindness, loving-kindness, His loving kindness, oh, how free!

2 When I can say, "My God is mine!"
When I can feel Thy glories shine,
I tread the world beneath my feet,
And all that earth calls good or great.

3 While such a scene of sacred joys
Our raptured eyes and souls employs,
Here we could sit and gaze away
A long, an everlasting day.

No. 112.   Responsive Service. Revive Us.

Opening Song — No. 27.

LEADER —

Wilt Thou not revive us again, that Thy people may rejoice in Thee?

CONGREGATION —

O Lord, revive Thy work in the midst of the years, in the midst of the years make known; in wrath remember mercy.

LEADER —

Though I walk in the midst of trouble, Thou wilt revive me.

CONGREGATION —

My heart shall rejoice in Thy salvation. I will sing unto the Lord, because He hath dealt bountifully with me.

LEADER —

Awake, thou that sleepest, and arise from the dead, and Christ shall give thee light.

CONGREGATION —

Awake! awake! put on thy strength, O Zion. Awake! as in the ancient days, in the generations of old.

LEADER —

Now it is high time to awake out of sleep: for now is our salvation nearer than when we believed.

CONGREGATION —

In Thee, O Lord, do I put my trust; let me never be put to confusion.

LEADER —

Wait on the Lord; be of good courage, and He shall strengthen thine heart.

Sing — No. 34, "We praise Thee," etc.

No. 113.   Responsive Service. Saved.

Opening Song — No. 2.

LEADER —

I am the door: by Me if any man enter in, he shall be saved, and shall go in and out, and find pasture.

CONGREGATION —

Who gave Himself for our sins, that He might deliver us from this present evil world, according to the will of God and our Father.

LEADER —

Except ye be converted, and become as little children, ye shall not enter into the kingdom of heaven.

CONGREGATION —

Not by works of righteousness which we have done, but according to His mercy He saved us, by the washing of regeneration, and renewing of the Holy Ghost.

LEADER —

For the Son of man is come to save that which was lost.

CONGREGATION —

I came not to judge the world, but to save the world.

LEADER —

For there is none other name under heaven given among men whereby we must be saved.

CONGREGATION —

He that endureth to the end shall be saved.

LEADER —

He shall deliver them from the wicked, and save them, because they trust in Him.

CONGREGATION —

He shall spare the poor and needy, and shall save the souls of the needy.

Sing — No. 40, "Depth of mercy."

No. 114. Praise Service.

Opening Song— Old Hundred, "Praise God, from whom all blessings flow."

LEADER—
I will praise the name of God with a song, and will magnify Him with thanksgiving.

CONGREGATION—
I will praise Thee, O Lord, with my whole heart; I will show forth all Thy marvelous works. I will be glad and rejoice in Thee: I will sing praise to Thy name, O Thou Most High.

LEADER—
Because Thou hast been my help, therefore in the shadow of Thy wings will I rejoice.
Sing — Verse 1, "Hail! great Creator," etc.

LEADER—
Ye that fear the Lord, praise Him; all ye the seed of Jacob, glorify Him; and fear Him, all ye the seed of Israel.

CONGREGATION—
The Lord is my strength and my shield; my heart trusted in Him, and I am helped: therefore my heart greatly rejoiceth; and with my song will I praise Him.
Sing — Verse 2, "At morning, noon," etc.

LEADER—
Let the people praise Thee, O God; let all the people praise Thee. Let the heaven and earth praise Him, the seas, and everything that moveth therein.

CONGREGATION—
O Lord, how manifold are Thy works! in wisdom hast Thou made them all: the earth is full of Thy riches.

LEADER—
The Lord thy God in the midst of thee is mighty; He will save. He will rejoice over thee with joy; He will rest in His love; He will joy over thee with singing.
Sing — Verse 3, "Thy glory beams," etc.

No. 115. St. Martin's.

Anon. WM. TANSUR, 1735

1. Hail! great Creator, wise and good! To Thee our songs we raise; Nature, thro' all.... her various scenes Invites us to Thy praise.

2 At morning, noon, and evening mild,
    Fresh wonders strike our view;
And, while we gaze, our hearts exult
    With transports ever new.

3 Thy glory beams in every star
    Which gilds the gloom of night;
And decks the smiling face of morn
    With rays of cheerful light.

116. (Key of G.)

I am coming to the cross;
 I am poor, and weak, and blind;
I am counting all but dross·
 I shall full salvation find.

Chorus.—I am trusting, Lord, in Thee,
 Blest Lamb of Calvary;
 Humbly at Thy cross I bow,
 Save me Jesus, save me now.

Long my heart has sighed for Thee,
 Long has evil reigned within.
Jesus sweetly speaks to me,—
 "I will cleanse you from all sin."

Here I give my all to Thee,—
 Friends, and time, and earthly store,
Soul and body,—Thine to be—
 Wholly Thine—for evermore.

In Thy promises I trust;
 Now I feel the blood applied;
I am prostrate in the dust;
 I with Christ am crucified.

117. (Key of F.)

Jesus, Lover of my soul,
 Let me to Thy bosom fly,
While the nearer waters roll,
 While the tempest still is high.
Hide me, O my Savior, hide,
 Till the storm of life is past;
Safe into the haven guide—
 Oh, receive my soul at last.

Other refuge have I none;
 Hangs my helpless soul on Thee;
Leave, oh, leave me not alone;
 Still support and comfort me.
All my trust on Thee is stayed;
 All my help from Thee I bring;
Cover my defenseless head
 With the shadow of Thy wing.

118. (Key of D.)

Sweet hour of prayer! sweet hour of prayer!
That calls me from a world of care,
And bids me at my Father's throne
Make all my wants and wishes known:
In seasons of distress and grief,
My soul has often found relief,
And oft escaped the tempter's snare,
By thy return, sweet hour of prayer!

weet hour of prayer! sweet hour of prayer!
Thy wings shall my petition bear
To Him whose truth and faithfulness
Engage the waiting soul to bless;
And since He bids me seek His face,
Believe His word, and trust His grace,
I'll cast on Him my every care,
And wait for thee, sweet hour of prayer.

119. (Key of G.)

Nearer, my God, to Thee,
 Nearer to Thee!
E'en though it be a cross
 That raiseth me,
Still all my song shall be,
Nearer, my God, to Thee!
 Nearer to Thee!

Though, like the wanderer,
 The sun gone down,
Darkness be over me,
 My rest a stone,
Yet in my dreams I'd be
Nearer, my God, to Thee,
 Nearer to Thee!

There let the way appear
 Steps unto heaven;
All that Thou send'st to me
 In mercy given;
Angels to beckon me
Nearer, my God, to Thee,
 Nearer to Thee!

120. (Key of F.)

What a Friend we have in Jesus,
 All our sins and griefs to bear;
What a privilege to carry
 Everything to God in prayer.
Oh, what peace we often forfeit,
 Oh, what needless pain we bear—
All because we do not carry
 Everything to God in prayer.

Have we trials and temptations?
 Is their trouble anywhere?
We should never be discouraged,
 Take it to the Lord in prayer.
Can we find a friend so faithful
 Who will all our sorrows share?
Jesus knows our every weakness,
 Take it to the Lord in prayer.

Are we weak and heavy laden,
 Cumbered with a load of care?
Precious Savior, still our refuge,—
 Take it to the Lord in prayer.
Do thy friends despise, forsake thee?
 Take it to the Lord in prayer;
In His arms He'll take and shield thee;
 Thou wilt find a solace there.

121. (Key of D.)

He leadeth me! oh, blessed thought!
Oh, words with heavenly comfort fraught!
Whate'er I do, where'er I be,
Still 't is God's hand that leadeth me.

Ref.—He leadeth me! He leadeth me!
 By His own hand He leadeth me;
 His faithful follower I would be,
 For by His hand He leadeth me.

Sometimes 'mid scenes of deepest gloom,
Sometimes where Eden's bowers bloom,
By waters still, o'er troubled sea,—
Still 't is His hand that leadeth me.

Lord, I would clasp Thy hand in mine,
Nor ever murmur or repine—
Content, whatever lot I see,
Since 't is my God that leadeth me.

122. (Key of G.)

My days are gliding swiftly by,
 And I, a pilgrim stranger,
Would not detain them as they fly,
 Those hours of toil and danger.

Cho.—For, oh! we stand on Jordan's strand;
 Our friends are passing over,
 And, just before, the shining shore
 We may almost discover.

Should coming days be dark and cold,
 We will not yield to sorrow,
For hope will sing, with courage bold,
 "There's glory on the morrow."

Let sorrow's rudest tempest blow,
 Each chord on earth to sever;
Our King says, "Come!" and there's our home
 Forever, oh, forever!

123.

(Key of E b.)

Just as I am, without one plea,
But that Thy blood was shed for me,
And that Thou bid'st me come to Thee,
. O Lamb of God! I come—I come!

Just as I am, and waiting not
To rid my soul of one dark blot,
To Thee, whose blood can cleanse each spot,
O Lamb of God! I come—I come!

Just as I am, though tossed about
With many a conflict, many a doubt,
Fightings within, and fears without,
O Lamb of God! I come, I come

Just as I am, poor, wretched, blind;
Sight, riches, healing of the mind,
Yea, all I need, in Thee to find,
O Lamb of God! I come—I come!

124

(Key of E b.)

The cross! the cross! the blood-stained cross!
The hallowed cross I see!
Reminding me of precious blood
That once was shed for me.

Chorus.—Oh, the blood! the precious blood
That Jesus shed for me,
Upon the cross, in crimson flood,
Just now by faith I see.

The cross! the cross! that heavy cross
My Savior bore for me;
It bowed Him to the earth with grief
On sad Mount Calvary.

The love! the love! the matchless love
That bled upon the tree!
It melts my heart, it wins my love,
It brings me, Lord, to Thee.

125

(Key of A b.)

Lord, I hear of showers of blessing
Thou art scattering full and free—
Showers the thirsty land refreshing;
Let some droppings fall on me.

Cho.—Even me, even me,
Let Thy blessings fall on me.

Pass me not, O gracious Father!
Sinful tho' my heart may be;
Thou might'st leave me, but the rather
Let Thy mercy fall on me.—Even me.

Pass me not, O tender Savior!
Let me love and cling to Thee;
I am longing for Thy favor;
Whilst Thou'rt calling, oh, call me!-Even me.

Pass me not! Thy lost one bringing,
Bind my heart, O Lord, to Thee;
While the springs of life are springing,
Blessing others, oh, bless me!—Even me.

126

(Key of A.)

Lord Jesus, I long to be perfectly whole;
I want Thee forever to live in my soul;
Break down every idol, cast out every foe;
Now wash me, and I shall be whiter than snow.

Chorus.—Whiter than snow, yes, whiter than snow;
Now wash me, and I shall be whiter than snow.

Lord Jesus, look down from Thy throne in the skies
And help me to make a complete sacrifice;
I give up myself and whatever I know—
Now wash me, and I shall be whiter than snow.

Lord Jesus, for this I most humbly entreat;
I wait, blessed Lord, at Thy crucified feet.
By faith, for my cleansing I see Thy blood flow—
Now wash me, and I shall be whiter than snow.

Lord Jesus, Thou seest I patiently wait;
Come now, and within me a new heart create;
To those who have sought Thee Thou never saidst no—
Now wash me, and I shall be whiter than snow.

127

(Key of G.)

My heavenly home is bright and fair;
Nor pain, nor death can enter there;
Its glittering towers the sun outshine;
That heavenly mansion shall be mine.

Cho.—I 'm going home, to die no more.

My Father's house is built on high,
Far, far above the starry sky;
When from this earthly prison free,
That heavenly mansion mine shall be.

Let others seek a home below
Which flames devour or waves o'erflow;
Be mine the happier lot to own
A heavenly mansion near the throne.

128

(Key of G.)

Father, I stretch my hands to Thee;
No other help I know;
If Thou withdraw thyself from me,
Ah! whither shall I go?

Cho.—I do believe, I now believe,
That Jesus died for me;
And thro' His blood, His precious blood,
I shall from sin be free.

What did Thine only Son endure,
Before I drew my breath!
What pain, what labor, to secure
My soul from endless death!

Author of faith, to Thee I lift
My weary, longing eyes;
Oh, may I now receive that gift—
My soul without it dies.

129.

(Key of E b.)

I hear the Savior say,
"Thy strength indeed is small;
Child of weakness, watch and pray,
Find in Me thine all in all."

Chorus.—Jesus paid it all,
All to Him I owe;
Sin had left a crimson stain,
He washed it white as snow.

For nothing good have I
Whereby His grace to claim—
I'll wash my garment white
In the blood of Calvary's Lamb.

When from my dying bed
My ransomed soul shall rise,
Then "Jesus paid it all"
Shall rend the vaulted skies.

130.

(Key of D.)

Joy to the world! the Lord is come!
Let earth receive her King;
Let every heart prepare Him room,
And heaven and nature sing.

Joy to the earth! the Savior reigns!
Let men their songs employ; [plains
While fields and floods, rocks, hills, and
Repeat the sounding joy.

No more let sins and sorrows grow,
Nor thorns infest the ground;
He comes to make His blessings flow
Far as the curse is found.

He rules the world with truth and grace,
And makes the nations prove
The glories of His righteousness
And wonders of His love.

131.

(Key of E b.)

There is a land of pure delight,
Where saints immortal reign;
Infinite day excludes the night,
And pleasures banish pain.

There everlasting spring abides,
And never with'ring flowers;
Death, like a narrow sea, divides
That heavenly land from ours.

Sweet fields, beyond the swelling flood,
Stand dressed in living green;
So to the Jews old Canaan stood,
While Jordan rolled between.

Oh, could we make our doubts remove,
The gloomy doubts that rise,
And see the Canaan that we love,
With unbeclouded eyes.

132.

(Key of G.)

Come, ye sinners, poor and needy,
Weak and wounded, sick and sore;
Jesus ready stands to save you,
Full of pity, love, and power.

Now, ye needy, come, and welcome,
God's free bounty glorify;
True belief and true repentance,
Every grace that brings you nigh.

Let not conscience make you linger
Nor of fitness fondly dream;
All the fitness He requireth
Is to feel your need of him!

Come, ye weary, heavy-laden,
Bruised and mangled by the fall;
If you tarry till you're better,
You will never come at all.

These words can be used with this chorus:

Cho.—Turn to the Lord, and seek salvation,
Sound the praise of His dear name;
Glory, honor, and salvation,
Christ, the Lord, is come to reign.

Or with the following:

Cho.—I will arise and go to Jesus;
He will embrace me in His arms;
In the arms of my dear Jesus,
Oh, there are ten thousand charms!

133.

(Key of G.)

Come, we that love the Lord,
And let our joys be known;
Join in a song with sweet accord,
And thus surround the throne.

Chorus.—We're marching to Zion,
Beautiful, beautiful Zion;
We're marching upward to Zion,
The beautiful city of God.

Let those refuse to sing
Who never knew our God;
But children of the heavenly King
May speak their joys abroad.

The hill of Zion yields
A thousand sacred sweets
Before we reach the heavenly fields
Or walk the golden streets.

Then let our songs abound,
And every tear be dry;
We're marching through Immanuel's ground
To fairer worlds on high.

INDEX.

TITLES IN SMALL CAPITALS.

A FOE IN THE LAND	10
A FRIEND INDEED	11
Again the Lord of life and light	25
Am I a soldier of the cross?	61
All hail the power of Jesus' name	1
ALL FOR JESUS	62
AS ONCE OF OLD	63
Away, away, o'er the ocean wave	20
Are you weary, are you heavy hearted?	103
BE NOT AFRAID	72
BEHOLD THE LAMB OF GOD	77
Blest be the tie that binds	88
BETHESDA	79
Break forth in melodies	65
Brethren, while we sojourn here	52
Brother, hast thou wandered	49
CALL THEM IN	2
Children of the heavenly King	73
CHRISTIAN'S BATTLE SONG	56
Christian, the Savior commands you	91
CHRISTIAN SOLDIERS	61
COME, THOU FOUNT	3
COME TO THE FOUNTAIN	13
COME WITH A MESSAGE	30
COME TO THE SABBATH SCHOOL	44
COME TO JESUS	47
Come weal, come woe	72
Come ye sinners, poor and needy	132
Come we that love the Lord	133
Come, Holy Spirit	94
COME HOME	52
Closer, dear Lord, to Thee	51
CONSECRATION (Responsive service)	105
CROWN HIM	1
Dear Savior, help me to be Thine	99
DENNIS	107
DEPTH OF MERCY	40
Down the wonderful tide	93
Father, I stretch my hands	128
FILL MY HEART WITH GLADNESS	51
FOLLOW HIM ALL THE WAY	91
FOR YOU AND FOR ME	78
GALILEE	82
GLORY TO JESUS	60
Grace, 't is a charming sound	107
GRACE (Responsive service)	106
Hail! great Creator	115
He leadeth me	121
HEAR THE SAVIOR CALLING	5
Hear the bugle sounding	27
HE KEEPETH ME EVER	75
HEAVEN FOR ME	50
HALLELUJAH FOR THE BLOOD	63
HELP ME, SAVIOR	99
Holy Father, we implore	105
HOME MISSION HYMN	23
How long, O Lord, how long	83
How precious the Lord to me	64
How sweet the cheering words	45
How tedious and tasteless the hours	14
I am coming to the cross	116
I hear the Savior say	129
I hear my Savior calling	35
I praise the Lord	50
I will give my heart	3
I WILL ARISE AND GO	35
I will try to be a soldier	37
IF I COME TO JESUS	67
If you want pardon	60
I 'M ALWAYS REJOICING	33
I 'M NEARER MY HOME	86
I 'm a soldier in the army	71
In the grey of early morning	68
I 'm behind the times	87
IT CAN NEVER BE TOLD	98
I WANT TO BE A WORKER	102
JESUS, MY TRUST	3
Jesus gives light in our sorrow	11
JESUS, SAVIOR OF THE WORLD	24
Jesus, Lover of my soul	117
JESUS, WE 'LL PRAISE THEE	80
Jesus is tenderly calling	55
JERUSALEM, MY GLORIOUS HOME	48
Joy to the world	130
Just as I am	123
JUST BESIDE THE RIVER	95
JESUS, I MY CROSS HAVE TAKEN	31
LIFT UP THE GATES	65
Little builders all are we	58
LORD, HELP ME	21
Lord! what a heaven	111
Lord, I hear of showers	125
Lord Jesus, I long to be perfectly	126
LOST! ALL LOST!	26
LOVING-KINDNESS	111
LOVE (Responsive service)	110
MAITLAND	109
Majestic sweetness sits enthroned	38
MILLENNIAL MORN	83
MUCH FORGIVEN	93
Must Jesus bear the cross alone	109
MY CITY	28
My days are gliding	122
My heart goes out	82
My heavenly home is bright	127
MY SURE FOUNDATION	6
My Christian friends in bonds	32
Nearer, my God, to Thee	119
Nearer to Thee, my Savior	6
No good-byes in heaven	81
NO OTHER FRIEND LIKE HIM	96
O Christian, the Savior commands	91
Oh, come to the fountain	16
Oh, come to the fountain	19
Oh, for a closer walk with God	85
Oh, for a thousand tongues	17
O HAPPY DAY	57
O Lord, my sin and guilt	79
O sinner, the Savior is calling	92
O precious, precious Jesus	96
Oh, sing to me of heaven	59

INDEX.

Oh, the white-robed throng	89
Oh, think of the home over there	18
Oh, what mercy flows	93
OH, YES; THERE'S SALVATION	43
ONWARD, CHRISTIAN SOLDIERS	90
PRAISE SERVICE	114
Praying there amid the	76
PRECIOUS PROMISES	64
Return, O wanderer, return	43
REVIVE US AGAIN	34
REVIVE US (Responsive service)	112
ROCK OF AGES	41
Rouse, ye Christian soldiers	56
SAFE ON THE SHINING STRAND	89
Saints rejoicing, angels	81
SALVATION IS FREE	92
SAVED (Responsive service)	113
SELF-CONSECRATION	84
SIMPLY TRUSTING	69
Since Christ, for sin	15
SINNER, HE CALLS THEE	55
Softly and tenderly Jesus is	78
STAND UP FOR JESUS	36
ST. MARTIN'S	115
Sweet are the promises	12
SWEETLY SAVED	39
Sweet hour of prayer	118
Take me, O my Father	84
TAKE MY HEART, DEAR JESUS	104
'TELL IT TO JESUS	103
THE STORY WILL NEVER GROW OLD	9
The half has never been told	9
THE WAY OF LIFE	15
THE WATER OF LIFE	16
THE FLOWING FOUNTAIN	19
THE WORD OF LIFE	20
THE CHRISTIAN ARMY	27
THE PARTING HAND	32
THE LORD IS MY SHEPHERD	42
The Sabbath school, O	44

THE WHOLE WIDE WORLD FOR JESUS	46
THE JASPER SEA	66
THE SAME SWEET STORY	70
THE RESURRECTION	68
THE TRANSFIGURATION	76
THE SINNER'S PLEA	74
The blood of Jesus cleanseth me	63
THE OLD-FASHIONED WAY	87
THE SINNER'S CALL	49
THE LITTLE BUILDERS	58
THE CROSS! THE CROSS!	124
There's an enemy at hand	10
There is a fountain	13
THERE AWAITS A CROWN	37
There is nothing in this	39
There is a land of pure delight	131
THERE'LL BE NO SORROW THERE	59
This is not my place	28
Thou Son of God	74
TO WHOM SHALL I GO?	7
Toiling on for Jesus	62
Thus the choir of angels	80
Thou thinkest, Lord, of me	101
Wave, wave the gospel banner	23
WELCOME MORN	25
We praise Thee, O God	34
WE SHALL MEET	64
We sing of Christ, our Savior	70
WE'RE GOING HOME	71
We speak of the realms	97
Weary, Lord, of struggling	31
What do you expect, my	2
What a Friend we have in	1
WHAT MUST IT BE TO BE THERE	57
WHERE HE LEADS I'LL FOLLOW	12
WHERE ARE YOUR TREASURES?	22
When our days of earthly	54
When we've crossed the	66
WHOSOEVER WILL	8
WHOEVER WILL	45
WILL THE WATERS BE CHILLY?	29
WORK (Responsive service)	108
When the King comes in	100

www.ingramcontent.com/pod-product-compliance
Lightning Source LLC
Chambersburg PA
CBHW020127170426
43199CB00009B/676